♡ Dedicated with love

    to our own children...
    ...and to all children everywhere
    who wish to be part
    of the world family of gardeners!

Susan
Jeff
Krista

Shelly
Melissa

Kurt
Lynn
Suzy

Celebrate the Seasons

A "Love Your Neighbor" Gardening Book

Linda Hunt
Marianne Frase
Doris Liebert

HERALD PRESS
Scottdale, Pennsylvania
Kitchener, Ontario

1983

Library of Congress Cataloging in Publication Data

Hunt, Linda, 1940-
    Celebrate the seasons.

    Includes index.
    Summary: A seasonal approach to gardening that
encourages the beginner to experience harmony with and
reverence for God's Earth. Includes instructions for
planning, planting, harvesting, recipes, and gifts
from the garden.
    1. Gardening-- Juvenile literature. [1. Gardening]
I. Frase, Marianne, 1935-   . II. Liebert, Doris,
    date-   . III. Title.
SB457. H86   1983   635'.024054   83-12657
ISBN 0-8361-3337-4   (pbk.)

CELEBRATE THE SEASONS

Copyright © 1983 by Herald Press, Scottdale, Pa. 15683
    Published simultaneously in Canada by Herald Press,
    Kitchener, Ont. N2G 4M5
Library of Congress Catalog Card Number: 83-12657
International Standard Book Number: 0-8361-3337-4
Printed in the United States of America

83   84   85   86   10   9   8   7   6   5   4   3   2   1

Contents

lettering
'n
ladybugs

by Marianne Frase

CELEBRATE the SEASONS

(A gardening book for kids who care)

Have you ever wanted to...

...share in the magic of seeing a small brown seed grow into a stem of colorful flowers or a bright orange pumpkin?

...or bite into a crisp green pea freshly picked from the vine?

Or have you ever wondered why neighbors or friends find such pleasure in tending their gardens?

Well, you're in good company!

I'm with you!

9

As long as there have been people
there have been gardens.
In every corner of the earth..

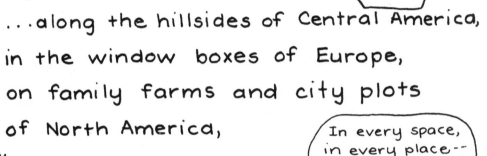

...along the hillsides of Central America,

in the window boxes of Europe,

on family farms and city plots

of North America,

In every space,
in every place--
even apartment
balconies!

you will see gardens being tended.

In the past, people had to garden for survival. Today, when many people no longer have to garden for all their food, they are gardening for other reasons.

Some are doing it...

...to save money

...for good health

...and for fun

and enjoyment!

Children, too, can join this worldwide family of gardeners.

During a season of gardening, you'll enjoy observing how something grows from seedtime to harvest

...and discovering how life is fragile-- needing tender care!

Hey! That's just like us!

Along with this you'll experience a closeness with the earth, and a feel for the changing seasons.

You'll also enjoy rewards for your efforts and the good feeling of participating in God's creation.

...and this book can help you!

Although most of us still depend on the supermarket for much of our food, more and more families are rediscovering the treasures of growing a home garden

They are gaining a new awareness of where food comes from and how it's produced. Some are choosing to eat local, seasonal crops and no longer expect to eat all fruits and vegetables regardless of the time of year.

Out-of-season crops require lots of energy to ship, process, and package!

AND...

They love the great taste of natural, fresh-picked, home-grown foods!

To become part of this worldwide family
of gardeners, let's look
at efforts we can make, some steps we can take.

We can start growing some of our own
food-- maybe with a friend. Being a producer
as well as a consumer adds a helpful link in
the food chain.

We can learn about gardens by talking to local experts -- friends, neighbors, and organizations in our community. We can ask our librarian to recommend books on the subject.

With tender care and special effort
the earth will provide us with wonder and
surprises...

   ...flowers to delight our hearts,
   and a generous variety of delicious
   foods to eat and share!

                              Sooo...

...here's a gardening book,

Celebrate <u>the</u> <u>Seasons</u>~

for kids who care!

Let's garden!

Garden Tools

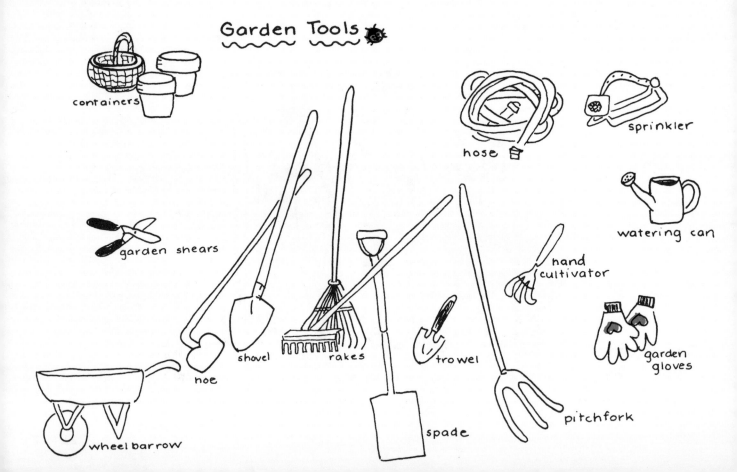

containers

hose

sprinkler

watering can

garden shears

hand cultivator

garden gloves

shovel

rakes

trowel

noe

spade

pitchfork

wheelbarrow

Gardening Terms

Bedding Plants (starter sets and seedlings)--Plants already started in nurseries are available to buy in springtime to be planted in your garden.

Potting Soil--Packaged and sold in bags--sterilized soil used for seedlings and container plants.

Fertilizer--Nutrients added to soil to encourage plant growth.

Compost--Natural fertilizer! Deposit kitchen wastes, grass clippings, and weeds into compost pile, and from it you receive rich, natural fertilizer.

Mulching--Placement of any material around plants to protect roots from heat, drought, and cold. (It's an effective weed controller.)

Gardening Terms...

Organic-- Any material that was once alive. (In gardening it refers to avoidance of chemicals.)

Thinning-- Removing enough plants so those remaining have enough room to spread leaves and roots.

Staking -- Supporting plants and vines to keep produce off the ground. Saves space and gives earlier harvest.

Pollenation -- Spreading of pollen from one plant to another by bees, butterflies, wind, birds, and water. Helps plants such as corn to grow properly.

Recycling-- Recovering something that has been thrown out and using it in another way.

I like turning trash into treasure!

What You Need:

a plan
a hopeful spirit

It's fun to garden with a friend!

WHERE TO PLANT?

Pick a place...

<u>Possibilities</u>--

part of a family garden,

patio container, window box,

or neighborhood plot --

(find a gardening partner,

join with friends, neighbors,

grandmas and grandpas).

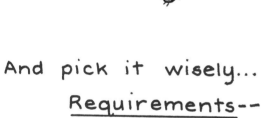

Some people are experimenting with solar greenhouses!

And pick it wisely...

Requirements--

    sunny spot - it needs at least

      6 hours of sunshine a day.

    access to water

    good soil--it will probably need

      your help (see page 39).

WHAT TO PLANT?

Possibilities--

Look through the seed catalogs
or visit a local nursery and check the
seed packet display.

After choosing your favorites
be a little daring and pick something
new!

Ever hear
of kohlrabi
or pak choy?

29

<u>Requirements</u>--

Now that you've dreamed your way through the catalogs and have planned a "farm" in your mind,

it's important to picture a garden that's realistic in size. A few well-cared-for plants will produce abundantly.

Gardens take time, so...

...think "small" if this is your first garden.

Small is beautiful!

Next, draw a picture of your garden and mark off different sections.

Remember -- gardens don't have to be in straight rows. You might try circles!

Some plants have special needs...

...such as pumpkins that gobble up space, and corn that grows best in double rows.

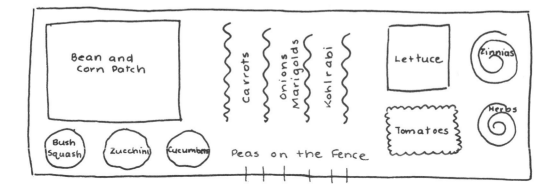

Community Gardens

Do you live in the city where there is not enough land for a vegetable garden? Don't despair, try joining a Community Garden! In many places, neighbors have gathered together and developed a donated vacant lot into a shared plot.

It's much more fun together!

Here each family has its own garden section, but often joins with others in the neighborhood for common tasks, such as plowing or fertilizing. This helps reduce expenses and makes the work easier and a lot more enjoyable. Sometimes these Community Gardens are sponsored by local organizations. Check with your county extension agent for one in your area.

Or if you don't have a garden spot, select containers in which to plant.

WHEN TO PLANT?

Possibilities--

Do your plants like cool or warm weather? Read the back of the seed packages to determine early and late plantings.

Check with your favorite expert to find out when crops like to be planted where you live.

A "When to Plant" Map

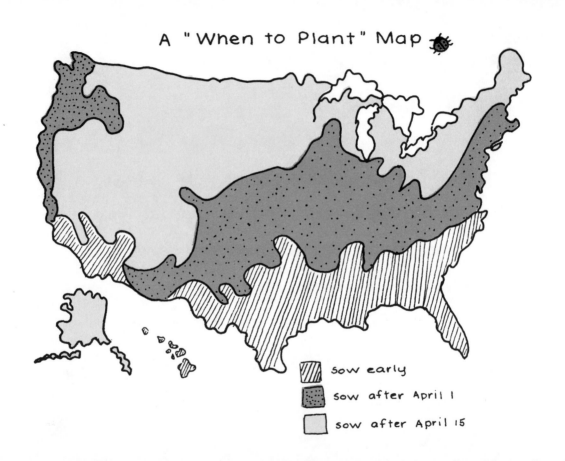

Sow early

Sow after April 1

Sow after April 15

36

What You Do:

 Choose seeds and starter sets.

 Make a home for your seeds by preparing the soil. Seeds need the right surroundings to grow into healthy plants.

To find out about your soil and what it needs, turn to the next page...

Plain brown dirt is often not good garden soil -- it usually needs your help!

Here's a little fun experiment for you!

I always wanted to be a scientist!

Ready...

How to Touch Test Your Soil Texture

Put a spoonful of soil in one hand, and add enough water so it is wet (not runny). Now work it with the other hand and rub it against your palm.

Clay soil will make your hands shiny and feel slippery.

Sandy soil will be dull and make your hands feel gritty.

You'll find watering hints for different soils on page 57.

Now you are ready to get set for planting.

How to Prepare Your Soil for Planting

Loosen the soil by soaking with water for several hours or until an inserted 8-inch stick is damp when pulled up.

Clear the ground of any weeds or grass.

Blanket with 2 or 3 inches of organic material (leaves, grass clippings, dried manure, compost, or packaged organic planting mix).

Add 1/4 inch manure or mulch.

Break up and turn over the soil (6 to 8 inches deep).

Smooth the soil with a rake until it is loose and soft.

Prepare the home for your seeds with lots of TLC ♥ (tender, loving care)!

Ready...
Get set...
GO!

Brr! It's too
cold outside!

Begin indoors for tender plants
(see page 54 on seedlings).

In certain climates some crops,
such as broccoli, need a head start.

Use jiffy pots and recyclable trays
and place near a sunny window.

Start outdoors with heartier plants and
cool weather crops.

These can include onion sets, potatoes,
root crops, leafy greens, and peas.

41

Use the following ideas to mark where you want to plant.

If planting in rows, try the "String Thing--Hoe Down".
Create even rows by driving stakes across from each other along the sides of your garden. Tie string to stake on one side, pull across the garden and tie to opposite stake. This will help your rows to be straight, and will show where the seeds have been planted so you won't accidentally walk on them.

Now place your hoe handle under the string and press it into the ground. Press gently if you need shallow rows; press harder if you need deeper rows.

If planting in circles or curved shapes, try "Hose Curls!"

Coil your garden hose to form the shape you want and press as you would with the hoe.

"String Thing--Hoe Down"

"Hose Curls"

Which will you choose?

43

You are finally ready to put the seeds and starter sets to bed.

Here are some helpful hints when planting seeds (leafy greens, peas, and root crops).

Iceberg Head Lettuce
Butter Head Lettuce
Romaine Lettuce
Red Lettuce

American Spinach
Swiss Chard

Carrots, short and long

Radishes

Parsnips

For your row planting:

Pour a few of the seeds into one hand and use your other hand to place the seeds carefully one by one into the ground. Be sure to space seeds far enough apart!

Use two hands, please!

For your curved plot--try a shaker!
Put your seeds in a container
with small holes in the top.
(An old-fashioned salt shaker
works great!)

Cover seeds with a thin blanket of
soil and sprinkle lightly with water.

HOW TO PLANT SPRING CROPS

Onion Sets

Begin with starter  sets from your local nursery.

Spanish Yellow
Bermuda White
Hamburger Red

Poke the bulbs, about 2 inches apart, into loosened soil until green tops are covered.

In 2 to 3 weeks your green onions will be ready to pull and use for salads. Pull every other onion. This is called "thinning" (see page 56).

Onion Sets...

Leave the remaining onions, now 4 inches apart, to grow throughout the summer.

When the tops begin to wither, dig up your onions, remove soil from the roots, and leave them to dry in the sunshine for a few days before storing.

Starter Sets

Potatoes

*(These need lots of space so be sure your garden is big enough before you start!)

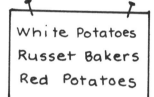

White Potatoes
Russet Bakers
Red Potatoes

Begin with healthy potatoes! It's important to use certified disease-free potatoes available at your local nursery.

Cut potatoes in quarters, leaving 2 eyes in each piece.

Dig 4-inch holes, 18 inches apart. Place 2 or 3 chunks with eyes facing up, in each hole. Cover.

 Potatoes...

Once there are flower-blossoms, you may gently dig for some of the tiny, new potatoes.

Yum! They're a special Spring taste treat!

Then mound dirt 3 to 4 inches higher to create room for the remaining potatoes to grow large.

When leaves turn yellow and die in late summer, big potatoes are ready to harvest.

Invite your friends for a "potato dig" and see how fast you can fill your basket! It's just like an Easter egg hunt!

Potatoes

VINE PEAS

Sugar Snap Peas
Snow Peas
Bush Peas

Begin by planting 2 inches deep and 2 inches apart. (If your soil is mostly clay, plant the seeds only 1 inch deep).

Save garden space by planting double rows 3 inches apart. Space these double rows 2½ feet apart.

After young plants grow 3 inches tall, thin them 4 to 6 inches apart (see page 56).

 Vine Peas...

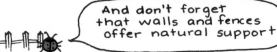
And don't forget that walls and fences offer natural support!

Now you need to stake the plants because vine peas can grow over 6 feet tall! Wow! Use two 6-foot stakes or poles (homemade or available at your nursery) and place on either side of your garden. String twine between the stakes and keep the vines tied to the string ladder. Using chicken wire between the stakes provides an excellent place for vines to climb. It can be rolled up at the end of the season and saved to use next year!

BUSH PEAS

Follow the first step for vine peas -- but plant rows 2 feet apart.

Also thin 4 to 6 inches apart.

"Pea-Picking"

Harvest young pea pods before they become tough and lose their bright green color.

Hold the vine in one hand while you pull the shell off with the other, to keep the tender vine from breaking.

And here's a happy surprise! The more you pick, the more your vine will give!

If you want your "pea-picking" to last longer, plant new crops every few days.

53

For those plants that need protection from cold spring weather, you may want to give them a head start indoors.

Seedlings take about 8 weeks to be strong enough for transplanting outdoors.

Look for Spring sales to buy your Jiffy-Pots and potting soil.

Fill your pots ½ inch from the top with soil and place on a large tray or pan. Using a pencil, poke 2 or 3 holes in the soil and drop a seed in each one. Cover gently with soil and sprinkle lightly. Label each pot.

Place the tray in a sunny window. In about a week sprouts will begin to appear. As you watch them grow be sure to keep the soil moist.

When the weather is frost-free, prepare your plants to be placed in the garden. Put your tray outdoors for several hours of sunshine, bringing it in at night. Do this for 3 or 4 days.

Now you are ready to put them in your garden plot or containers.

 Thinning

As your plants grow larger, they will begin to crowd each other. Pull out some of the plants to give the others more space to grow big and healthy. This is called "thinning." Your seed packet will tell you how far apart to thin different plants.

Ouch! Too tight!

Ahh! Just right!

Watering

 Different plants have different watering needs, so you must consider your own climate and soil when deciding how much to water. Sandy soil, which drains rapidly, needs watering more often than clay. It takes a long time for water to get

through clay soil-- but you don't have to water it as often. A deep soaking is always better than frequent light waterings.

You won't have to water again until the top few inches of soil are dry!

A Container Assortment

You don't need yard space to have a garden. With imagination you can turn almost any container into a home for your vegetables and flowers.

Go on a scavenger hunt looking for containers that will hold soil and water and are at least 9 inches deep. Some ideas might be a barrel cut in half, an old laundry tub, reusable plasticware and pottery, even a castaway toy box or suitcase.

Gather together some small stones, potting soil, seeds, or seedlings.

Containers need a way for the water to drain. If your container doesn't have holes you will want to make some. A small pot requires only one hole while larger containers may need more.

Now you are ready to add the small stones. Put them in a layer across the bottom of your container. This will help the water to drain more easily.

Fertilize! A variety of fertilizers are available. Use according to directions.

Set your container in a sunny place-- on the patio, porch, deck, staircase, or in a window box -- and watch your garden grow!

You'll love containers! Few pests or weeds will bother!

Add potting soil to within one inch from the top. Then plant your seeds and seedlings.

Water regularly, as needed, depending on your climate. The type and size of the container you use will determine how often.

Container plants need "E S A" (extra special attention) -- so be alert!

When the soil is dry to the touch, it needs water!

Herb Garden

"celebrate the seasonings!"

   Plant herbs in small containers to grow on your patio. They can be moved indoors in winter. You can also plant them in groups in your garden plot. Favorite cooks on your list will love them for gifts (see page 160).

Peppermint
Mint
Dill
Oregano
Thyme
Sage

You might want to try some others!

PARSLEY

Parsley grows quickly from seed. Its bright green leaves perk up and garnish foods.

CHIVES

Purchase plantings in springtime. Because Chives are perennials, they'll come up year after year if you plant them in your garden.

What You Get:

a time of watching the miracle
of seeds changing into tender green leaves
as they push through the earth,
beginnings, delicate nibbles,

something for here and now...

...and the promise of more to come!

SPRING'S EARLY DELIGHTS

Recipes

Surprise Spring Pie

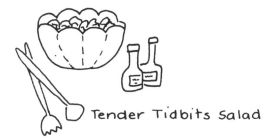

Tender Tidbits Salad

Tender Tidbits Salad

What You Need:

> thinnings--
>   (spinach, lettuce, radishes)
> your favorite salad dressing
> serving bowl

Try this when your shoots need trimming!

What You Do:

1. Gather your garden thinnings.

2. Rinse salad pieces gently, then pinch off roots and stems.

3. Place in bowl and toss with your favorite dressing!

What You Get:
A once-a-year delicacy!

My favorite is just plain Rice Vinegar (seasoned gourmet type)! Delicious!

Surprise Spring Pie

It's Popeye's favorite pie!

What You Need:

2 cups chopped spinach
1/3 cup chopped green onions
1 cup shredded swiss cheese
2 cups milk
4 eggs
1 cup unbleached flour
1½ teaspoons baking powder
½ teaspoon salt
⅛ teaspoon pepper
2 Tablespoons melted butter
(or margarine)

9" pie plate

What You Do:

1. Wash spinach and chop leaves coarsely to make 2 cups.

2. Chop the green onions and shred the cheese.

3. Sprinkle spinach, onion, and then cheese in the bottom of a greased pie plate.

4. In a large bowl, beat or blend the rest of the ingredients and pour mixture over the spinach, onions, and cheese.

5. Bake 35-40 minutes in a 400° oven.

6. Allow to set for 5 minutes before serving.

<u>What</u> <u>You</u> <u>Get</u>:

A tasty main dish pie that makes its own crust and serves 6!

Summer

What You Need:

...frost-free weather
a working spirit

It's time
to plant
and protect!

Let's roll up
our sleeves and
get to work!

What You Do:

In the spring we prepared the soil. Now it's time to plant and protect summer crops.

HOW TO PLANT SUMMER CROPS

Jack would love it up here!

Beans

POLE BEANS

Kentucky Wonder
Romano
Yellow Snap
Golden Crop

Begin by planting 1 inch deep and 3 inches apart. Save garden space by planting double rows 3 feet apart.

After young plants grow 3 inches tall, thin 6-10 inches apart.

Now you will need to stake the plants because pole beans can grow up to 8 feet tall!

As with vine peas, use stakes and twine or chicken wire to support vines as they climb (see page 51).

Or create a bean-pole tepee for a shady summer hideaway by placing stakes in a circle and securing at the top with twine.

I like to pick the beans from inside!

BUSH BEANS

Follow the first step for pole beans -- but plant rows 2 feet apart.

Thin young seedlings 4-6 inches apart.

"Bean Brigade"

Help! The beans are coming!

Beans grow <u>very</u> quickly so gather your friends and baskets and get ready for an abundant harvest! Pick beans while they are young and tender and you will be rewarded with enough beans for your family, and lots to share!

Standard Sweet Corn
White Corn
Popcorn
Ornamental Corn
(Long Rainbow-
     Short Strawberry)

Corn
=====

Choose a place in your garden where tall corn stalks will not shade other garden crops.

With the "hoe-down" method (see page 42), mark four rows side by side -- two feet apart.

Corn needs lots of hot summer sun!

Plant seeds 1 inch deep, and 4-6 inches apart.

Corn

Planting corn in four rows rather than in a single long row helps pollenation, providing healthy kernels.

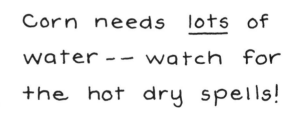

When young plants are 6 inches tall, thin 8 – 12 inches apart.

Corn needs <u>lots</u> of water -- watch for the hot dry spells!

"Corn Cob Peek and Pull"

Before harvesting corn, peek before you pull.

Your first clue that corn is ripe comes in the late summer when the silky tassels on the ears begin to turn brown.

Check often! In hot weather corn can go quickly from tender to tough!

Peek inside the corn husk to test a kernel. Pop it with your thumbnail. If <u>clear</u> juice squirts out, the corn is not ready. When the juice is <u>milky</u> it is ripe to pull.

Pull the corn and cook it as soon as possible for fantastic flavor!

Cucumbers

Bush Cucumbers
(space savers)
Salad Cucumbers
Pickling Cucumbers
Lemon Cucumbers

Make a hilltop home for. your seeds by shaping dirt into 2 - foot - wide mounds.

Evenly space 5-6 seeds ½ inch deep in each hill.

Because traveling vines spread, hills need to be 4 - 5 feet apart.

Cucumbers can also climb trellises if your garden spot is small!

Cucumbers...

When seedlings are 6-8 inches tall, select your 3 strongest plants. Pull out the others to thin.

Cucumbers become bitter when they stay on the vine too long, so pick them while they are young.

Lemon cucumbers are my favorite!

Pumpkins

Jack-o-Lantern
Big Max
   (for Halloween
   and County Fairs)
Small Sugar
   (for pies and
   cooking)

Make large hilltop homes by mounding dirt 2 feet wide, 6 – 8 feet apart.

Evenly space 5- 6 seeds 1 inch deep in each hill.

Thin to your 2 strongest plants after shoots are 6- 8 inches high.

Liebert's Log Cabin

JM

"The earth, O Lord,
is full of thy
steadfast love..."

Pumpkins...

Harvest for Halloween -- just in time for jack-o-lanterns and delicious pumpkin pies!

Rinse and dry pumpkin seeds -- some for roasting now and others for planting your pumpkin patch next summer!

SUMMER SQUASH

It's a sure winner!

Early White Bush *
Golden Crookneck
Zucchini

*Be sure to try this--
it looks like a spaceship!

Squash

Build hilltop homes as you did with cucumbers and pumpkins, only place them 3-4 feet apart, evenly spacing 4-6 seeds in each mound.

Thin to your 3 strongest plants when the shoots are 6 inches tall.

You'll always feel like a super gardener when you harvest your summer squash because it is such a plentiful and fast-growing crop.

You'll want to check your plants daily for ideal size as recommended on the individual seed packets.

FALL and WINTER SQUASH

Butternut Squash
Acorn Squash
Spaghetti Squash
Ornamental Gourds

For planting and thinning bush squash, follow directions for summer squash.

For vine-type squash, do the same, except space hills 6-8 feet apart. Like pumpkins, these squash grow best in soil with plenty of compost.

Pick before a hard frost, leaving the stem attached to the fruit.

Store in a cool, dry place where your squash will wait for Thanksgiving dinner.

You'll find the recipe for Spaghetti Squash on page 128, a tasty treat!

Tomatoes

Early Girl
Beefsteak
Patio Cherry
Yellow Plum

Begin with young tomato plants from your local nursery.

Dig a hole deep enough so half the stem is buried. Place 18 inches apart-- in rows 3-4 feet apart.

Tomatoes...

When the plants are 12 inches high, tie them to a stake, chicken wire, fence, or use tomato cages (handy, inexpensive, and reusable).

tomato cages

Tomatoes love lots of water and sun. For a bountiful crop add extra fertilizer when plants begin to bloom.

Tomatoes...

Tomato harvesting brings special pleasure.
There is nothing like the taste of a
juicy, red tomato warmed by
the summer sun!

Pick when firm and
ripe red.

Color Check

Be patient!
Bright red
is best!

Flowers--Scattered Jewels

"No-Fail Flowers"
- Marigolds
- Zinnias
- Strawflowers
- Snap Dragons
- Phlox

Flowers brighten our spirits, giving whimsy and beauty to the garden. As you work, your flowers are working with you (see page 98).

Intersperse flowers, especially marigolds, around your garden border, or create pockets of color within it.

Most flowers grow well from seed, but follow planting directions on your seed packet carefully. You might want to get a head start by using bedding plants.

Garden helpers

Borrow from the British!

Try an old-fashioned English country garden in one of your "pockets." Enjoy the surprises that come with this kaleidescope of color, size, and shape. Just open the packet and sprinkle seeds in your prepared bed. Cover, and wait for the sparkling gems' to appear!

"For lo, the winter is past,
the rain is over and gone.
The flowers appear on the earth..."

Remember, you can enhance every corner with colorful floral jewels by placing them in containers (see page 59).

Sunflowers -- The Edible Flower

No garden is complete without this giant "sunburst on stilts"! Each sunny face brims with personality as it stands tall, cheering your garden. In the fall you have the added benefit of eating its delicious, crunchy seeds.

It's nutritious too!

To harvest, cut off sunflower heads and set aside to dry for 2-3 weeks. To remove seeds, rub heads against each other, or rub over a wire mesh screen. Spread seeds out on a tray or baking sheet until dry.

Now they are ready to roast (see page 145).

HOW TO PROTECT YOUR CROPS

Frost Warnings

In early summer the weather report may warn of frost and you will need to protect fragile plants.

Gently cover them to keep them warm overnight. Remove covering in the morning when the danger is over.

Brr! This will keep them from freezing!

You may use milk cartons, cans, newspapers, or plastic sheeting--just a few of many possibilities.

Weed Watch

Weeds try to crowd out growing plants, robbing your vegetables of needed food and water.

Catch weeds early -- while they are still small. It's easier to pull out the entire weed, including the root, before it is firmly imbedded in the ground.

Take advantage of a rainfall which softens the soil and makes weeding less work.

Weeding after a thorough watering is also helpful!

Be careful not to pull out precious plants when you weed!

Mulch Magic

After plants are 6 inches tall, try mulching. Mulching means covering the soil around your plants with straw, leaves, old rotted sawdust, grass clippings, or other organic material.

Mulching gives a great boost to the garden!
It helps keep weeds from growing.
It helps keep water in the soil.
It helps keep the earth at
an even temperature.

weeds

Pest Control

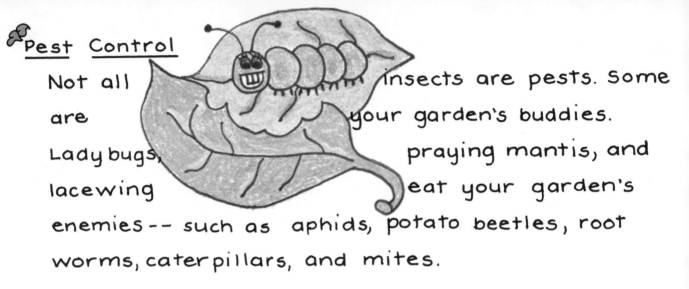

Not all insects are pests. Some are your garden's buddies. Ladybugs, praying mantis, and lacewing eat your garden's enemies -- such as aphids, potato beetles, root worms, caterpillars, and mites.

Take advantage of the natural friends of your garden-- flowers and these helpful insects. Some flowers attract helper insects, while others, such as marigolds, with their unusual scent, discourage troublesome pests.

If possible, avoid using chemical sprays which keep "garden patrollers" away.

If pests persist, try this homemade remedy:

> Stir ¼ cup liquid dish detergent into
>   1 quart water.
> Spray or sprinkle on your plants.

Water Works

Hot summer sun makes plants thirsty. When well watered, plants flourish. Without enough water, they wither and die.

"Flourishing Flora"

"Withering wilties"

A thorough soaking is better than quick sprinkles.

♪ Planting, staking, weeding, raking-- a garden making! ♪

A scarecrow can be a fun addition to your vegetable patch. Some believe garments flapping in the wind really scare away birds or small animals that like to nibble at tender leaves and plants. Don't be disappointed if it just provides a friendly perching place for the local birds!

What You Get:

...the wonder of seeing and tasting,
continuing amazement at nature's
variety and abundance,
and the fun of sharing the rewards of the
work you have done!

I like sharing
with my friends
and the local
food bank!

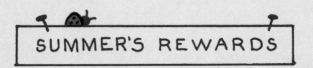

SUMMER'S REWARDS

Recipes

Vegie Stir-Fry

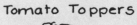

Tomato Toppers

Fresh Bean Salad

Zucchini Muffins

Vegie Stir-Fry

What You Need:

> 1 Tablespoon vegetable oil
> 1 chopped green pepper
> 1 chopped onion
> 2 cups snow peas
> 10 chopped mushrooms
> 1 Tablespoon soy sauce
>
> large skillet

What You Get:

4 servings of tasty, crisp vegetables!

What You Do:

1. Heat oil in a large skillet over medium heat.

2. Chop green pepper, onion, and mushrooms.

3. Cook green pepper and onion in oil until tender. Add peas and mushrooms and stir for 3-4 minutes.

4. Add soy sauce and serve!

Cook until tender-- but still crisp!

Tomato Toppers

Choose tomatoes that are large and firm. Cut in halves. Top each tomato half with one of the following:

1. Cottage cheese-- sprinkle with parsley sprigs, chives, or paprika.

2. Egg salad
   Chop 2 hard-boiled eggs. Add a tablespoon of mayonnaise, salt and pepper to taste, ¼ teaspoon dry mustard, and chopped parsley or pickles.

Serve your "topped tomatoes" on a bed of crisp lettuce!

3. Tuna fish salad
   Mix 1 small can tuna with ¼ cup yogurt.

Zucchini Muffins

What You Need:

3 eggs
1¼ cups sugar
1 cup vegetable oil
3 teaspoons vanilla
2 cups grated zucchini
(unpeeled)
2 Tablespoons grated orange rind
3 cups unbleached flour
1 teaspoon salt
1 teaspoon baking soda
¼ teaspoon baking powder
2 teaspoons cinnamon

2 12-cup muffin tins
24 muffin papers

What You Do:

1. In a large bowl, beat eggs.

2. Add sugar and beat a little more.

3. Add oil, vanilla, zucchini, orange rind -- and beat.

4. Add flour, salt, baking soda, baking powder, cinnamon, and stir until mixed.

Zucchini Muffins

5. Place muffin papers in muffin tins and fill half full with batter.

6. Bake muffins at 325° for 25 minutes.

What You Get:

24 marvelous muffins-- delicious with honey!

 # Grilled Corn-on-the-Cob

Be sure to try this on your next picnic or camping trip!

What You Need:

fresh ears of corn
   (in the husks)
butter or margarine
salt

campfire, grill

What You Get:

Tender and delicious corn – ready to eat right on the cob!

What You Do:

1. Pull husk down on each ear of corn and carefully remove the "hair" (cornsilk).
2. Pull husk back up and soak ears in cold water for 15-30 minutes.
3. Place ears (in husks) on grill and cook 15-20 minutes.
4. When the inside steams and the outer husk is dry and turning brown, the corn is done.
5. Remove husks to serve. Spread with butter and salt to enjoy this outdoor treat.

Try this with Fresh Fried Fish

Fresh Bean Salad

What You Need:

2 cups cooked green beans
2-3 Tablespoons French dressing
(Choose your favorite!)

onion rings, thinly sliced
Parmesan cheese
covered saucepan
covered serving dish

What You Get:

A cool summer salad
that serves 4!

What You Do:

1. Wash beans and cut in bite-sized pieces.

2. Cook until tender in a covered saucepan with ½ cup water. Drain.

3. When beans are cool, stir in dressing and refrigerate overnight in a covered dish.

4. At serving time stir in 1-2 tablespoons cheese and garnish with onion.

What You Need:

...searching eyes
working hands
a faithful spirit

Searching eyes... to find those vegetables which play hide-and-seek in fall's dense foliage. You need to be a "super-sleuth" as you harvest your garden.

Working hands... to continue summer's care of watering and weeding and autumn's task of gathering bountiful rewards.

A faithful spirit... to match your garden's
generous outpouring,
    and a willingness to harvest
        every day!

Carrots

What You Do:

 Continue summer's care of watering and weeding.

 Visit your garden daily with a basket in hand for a harvest hunt. Squash, cucumbers, and tomatoes often hide beneath the leaves and vines. Search with alert eyes!

"The earth has yielded its increase; God our God has blessed us..."

Listen to weather reports for frost-alerts. Warm Indian summer days sometimes will be followed with surprise attacks from Jack Frost. Some of your plants-- especially tomatoes-- will need to be covered with sheeting of some sort, or picked to prevent damage from freezing.

Store winter-keeping vegetables in grocery bags or boxes in a cool, dry place. Carrots and parsnips should be put in plastic bags and kept in the refrigerator.

Restore your garden plot for next year's plantings. Fall-keeping includes cleaning out and revitalizing the garden.

Everything goes during "Fall Clearance" time! Pull, pluck, and yank all vines or withered growth and toss into waiting wheelbarrows or boxes.

Replenish the soil by digging in the leftover mulch or additional organic fertilizer.

And save the cornstalks for your Thanksgiving celebration (see page 134).

Fall is the time to begin a compost pile for next summer's garden if you don't already have one.

Compost -- The Gardener's Gold

For years organic gardeners around the world have shown the wisdom of recycling nature's "leftovers" back into the soil. This adds rich nutrients to speed growing plants. The process of preparing and turning "worthless" garbage into garden gold is called composting.

Compost...

Natural, rich compost is something you can't buy at a store. You have to make it!

Build an uncovered bin outdoors or use a garbage can.

Like a submarine sandwich, layer 3 levels of organic materials into a pile.

1st level-- Vegetable materials.
Includes grass clippings, leaves, twigs, kitchen garbage (no bones or meat).
2nd level-- Manure (buy it at a nursery).
3rd level-- Soil.

Soil
Manure
Vegetable materials

Compost can

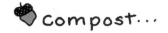 Compost...

Put a few inches of each layer in your bin.
Sprinkle with water, and leave to decay.

Over the months, occasionally turn with a
pitchfork, and sprinkle with water.
The organic material will decay into
a rich, dark humus called compost.
You can add new layers of the 3
levels from time to time.

There are other
compost methods
and hints! Check
with your
favorite local
organic gardener!

If you begin in the fall, your compost will
be ready in the spring. Then you can add
it to the garden. Mix it into your soil and
watch your plants smile!

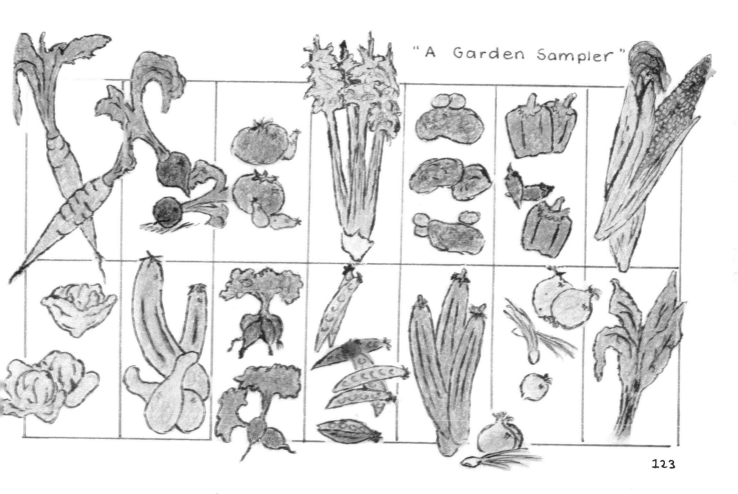

"A Garden Sampler"

123

Reward hardworking tools, your partners in the garden, with extra-special attention by cleaning and storing carefully.

You'll be glad you did!

And don't forget those reusable props-- stakes, coverings, tomato cages, chicken wire, etc. Then they'll be ready and waiting for next year's garden!

What You Get:

Gifts from the garden for all the days...

...home-cooked meals on frosty nights, foods and natural decorations for festive celebrations.

And thankful hearts for the "movable feast"!

. . . . .The Movable Feast. . . .

Gather your harvest in wagons and
bushel baskets and move your
treasures inside
to be transformed
into a feast for
eye and table!

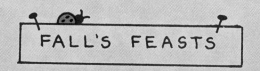

FALL'S FEASTS

Recipes

Pumpkin Stew

Stuffed Potato Boats

Harvest Decorations

Spaghetti Squash

Spaghetti Squash

What You Need:

> 1 spaghetti squash
> butter or margarine
> salt and pepper
>
> 13" x 9" shallow pan

It's funny
for your tummy!

What You Do:

1. Ask an adult to cut the squash in half lengthwise.

2. Scoop out the seeds.

3. Place the squash halves cut side down in a shallow pan and fill with ½ inch water.

4. Cook at 350° approximately one hour or until tender when tested with a fork.

Spaghetti Squash

5. Remove pan carefully from oven.

6. Turn squash back over with a spatula being careful not to burn yourself. Cut in wedges, add a dab of butter and salt and pepper to taste.

What You Get:

Yummy, squiggly squash that looks just like spaghetti!

Pumpkin Stew

What You Need:

> 1 pumpkin
> (as big as a serving bowl)
> 1 cup chopped onion
> ½ cup chopped green pepper
> 2 Tablespoons vegetable oil
> 1½ pounds lean ground beef
> 1 teaspoon salt, dash pepper
> 1 bay leaf
> 4 cups chicken broth
> (or bouillon)
> 2 cups rice
> 1 Tablespoon margarine
>
> cookie sheet
> electric fry pan
> (or large skillet)

What You Do:

(PREPARING THE PUMPKIN)

1. Get help with slicing off the top of the pumpkin, and scooping out the seeds and stringy pulp.

2. Rinse, and sprinkle with salt and pepper.

3. Put top back on and bake on cookie sheet for 1 hour at 350°

While pumpkin bakes you can prepare stew filling!

(PREPARING THE FILLING)

4. Heat oil in skillet. Add onions, green pepper, meat, and spices. Cook until brown.

5. Add broth to skillet. When mixture comes to a boil, add rice and margarine.

6. Turn heat down to low, put on lid, and simmer for 15 minutes.

7. Place mixture in baked pumpkin shell.

8. Return pumpkin to oven and continue baking for 15 minutes so that flavors mingle.

It's a pumpkin plus!

<u>What</u> <u>You</u> <u>Get</u>:
A fun and zesty harvest
stew that serves 6-8!

Stuffed Potato Boats

What You Need:

3 potatoes, already baked

⅓ cup milk

3 Tablespoons butter
or margarine

dash of salt, pepper

1 Tablespoon chopped
green onions or
parsley

½ cup shredded cheese

bits of leftover meat
or mushrooms, etc.

Paprika

shallow baking pan

What You Do:

Next time you bake potatoes, save energy and put in a few extra to make these "boats" for another meal. I like to use leftovers for this recipe!

1. Bake potatoes in a 400° oven for one hour after scrubbing them well and pricking each one with a fork.

2. Cut cooled potatoes in halves lengthwise.

3. Scoop out potato from shell and mash in a bowl with butter, milk, salt, and pepper.

4. Add cheese, green onions, or parsley and any bits of leftover meat you might have. (Mushroom pieces are also a good addition!)

5. Fill potato shells heaping full with mixture and sprinkle with paprika.

6. Place on baking sheet and heat your "boats" at 400° for 20-25 minutes -- until hot and golden brown.

Yum! These melt in your mouth!

<u>What</u> <u>You</u> <u>Get</u>:

Six "melt-in-your-mouth" boats for a fall supper!

Harvest Decorations

Hi!

Welcome guests at your door with...
...a colorful hanging of dried corn husks, strawflowers, and dried weeds--tied together with a bright ribbon.

Add cornstalks placed next to your door with a few pumpkins for color!

Your harvest table will look festive with...
...a basket piled high with gourds of various colors and sizes, or a cornucopia spilling over with your garden's rewards!

Add some fall leaves for a nice touch!

Winter

What You Need:

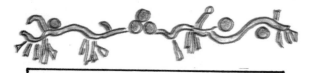

a rest for the garden!
a rest for you!
a giving spirit

It's "R and R" time! (Rest and renewal time!)

Your garden has been abundantly producing, and now the earth needs a time of rest and renewal.

You too have been working hard all year, and probably need to put gardening aside for a time. This is natural.

Winter offers quietness in nature's seasonal cycle.

What You Do:

 Transform your garden treasures into delightful presents--
wrap, tie with ribbon, and give with love!

This time of rest in winter provides a chance to create gifts from the garden for the season's festive moments.

You and your garden can continue to give-- even in the winter!

Grandparents, neighbors, and friends all love thoughtful, homemade presents and your garden has given you transformable treasures.

So here are some ideas to start you off. Your own imagination will help you think of others! (Projects begin on page 144.)

Hey! It's made by me!

by Me!

Think ahead! Order your new seed catalogs (see page 162) and browse through the tempting pictures of colorful vegetables and flowers.

Think back on your last summer's garden, remembering what you liked best about it -- AND what was disappointing to you. Before you plan next summer's garden you might ask yourself some questions.

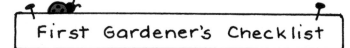

First Gardener's Checklist

What grew best in your garden?

What tasted most delicious to you?

...to your pests?

Did you plant too much?

What plants gave you problems?

Did your "plan" allow enough space for each crop?

Did too much need to be harvested at once?

A first garden is like your first try at anything! The more you work at it, the more confident and successful you'll become.

Do you remember when you first tried riding a bicycle or playing a musical instrument? You may have felt discouraged in the beginning. You may have had some similar moments as a new gardener-- your favorite vegetable didn't come up or your tomatoes didn't ripen.

Experience is the best teacher!

Take heart!
With time and practice your garden will get better
and   better!

What You Get:

The joy of giving gifts from your garden,
a change of pace -- to give you renewed
enthusiasm
...and a time to dream about
next year's garden!

WINTER'S WONDERS

Gifts from the Garden

Strawflower Bouquet

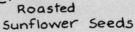

Roasted Sunflower Seeds

Recycled Christmas Tree

Potato Print Wrap

Corn Husk Tree Trims

Herbs

Pressed Flower Presents

Paper-white Narcissus

Roasted Sunflower Seeds

What You Need:

4 cups sunflower seeds
¼ cup salt
6 cups water
saucepan
cookie sheet

What You Get:

A delightful crunchy treat for your friends. (Don't forget to save a few for your bird friends too!)

What You Do:

1. Place seeds, salt, and water in saucepan and boil 5 minutes.

2. Drain and spread on paper towels to dry.

3. Place on cookie sheet and bake 25-30 minutes. Stir once.

4. Store in a dry place.

For gifts, fill a variety of small jars with seeds and tie a ribbon around them!

145

Pressed Flower Presents

Create your own cards, bookmarks, and pictures!

What You Need:

collection of simple flowers
    from your garden and
    wild flowers from the field
blotting paper
heavy books
paper for card, cut to size
clear plastic wrap
felt-tip pen
craft glue
tape

What You Do:

1. Arrange flowers on a sheet of blotting paper so that they don't touch each other. Place another sheet on top.

2. Put several heavy books over them for 3-4 weeks.

3. When dry, arrange flowers on your prepared paper.

You may want to write a message first!

4. Glue flowers on paper carefully.

5. Cut plastic wrap a little larger than paper and cover your entire card or picture.

6. Smooth plastic wrap, folding the extra to back of card, and taping the corners.

7. Your pressed flower picture is ready to use as is, or may be put in a frame or envelope.

It's for you!

What You Get:

A gift picture, personalized bookmark, or card!

Corn Husk Tree Trims

("Heart-in-a-Wreath" and Chains)

You'll love these! ♥

What You Need:

dried corn husks
1 Tablespoon glycerine
   in 1 quart of water
red construction paper
½ inch red-and-white-
   check ribbon
white thread, needle
stapler
scissors
craft glue

heart pattern
(see next page)

What You Do:

1. Soak dried husks in a quart of water with glycerine until they are soft and easy to bend.

2. Cut lengthwise into 3/4-1-inch-wide strips.

3. You will need the longest strip to make the "heart-in-a-wreath" ornament. Save the others for chains.

4. Bend the longest strip to form a circle about 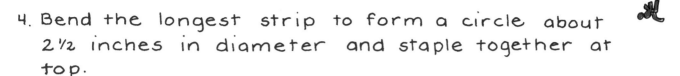 2½ inches in diameter and staple together at top.

5. Trace a pattern from the heart at the bottom of the page. Use the pattern to cut 2 red construction paper hearts.

6. Fold each heart in half and with just a small amount of craft glue join the 2 hearts, back to back, on the fold. Hold until dry and then open slightly to form a 3-dimensional heart.

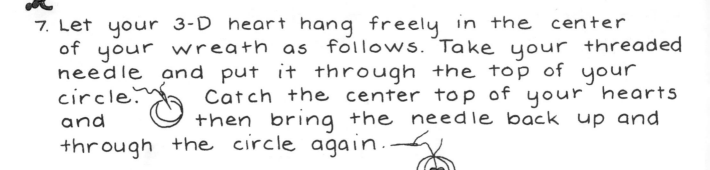

7. Let your 3-D heart hang freely in the center of your wreath as follows. Take your threaded needle and put it through the top of your circle. Catch the center top of your hearts and then bring the needle back up and through the circle again.

8. Leave enough thread on both ends above wreath to make a hanger. Tie a bow around the hanger, knot the thread ends, and your ornament is ready for the tree!

Lovely!

150

And now,

 chains...

9. Use the shorter lengths of husk strips you saved to make natural chains to go on the tree. Form chain by bending the wet strips into circles and connecting them by stapling the ends together.

<u>What You Get</u>:

Lovely natural ornaments for your tree -- or a friend's!

And you'll have fun making them too!

Paper White Narcissus

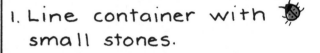
You'll love these beautiful fresh flowers that bring a promise of spring to brighten cold winter days!

What You Need:

6-8 paper-white narcissus bulbs
collection of small stones
shallow container

What You Get:

Beautiful blooms to give to someone special!

What You Do:

1. Line container with small stones.

2. Place bulbs on top of stones.

3. Cover with water.

4. Set in sunny window for 6 weeks.

Strawflowers Bouquet

What You Need:

Strawflowers
florist wire
2 feet ribbon

What You Do:

1. Harvest strawflowers before heads are fully developed.

2. Remove foliage leaves and bunch loosely.

3. Hang flowers with head downward in a cool airy place to dry slowly.

You might want to add some wild baby's breath to your bouquet!

Strawflowers Bouquet...

4. When dry, remove the stems. Use florist wire to poke into center of each flower.

5. Gather stems together with colorful ribbon to create a bouquet.

What You Get:

An ideal gift --
an everlasting
bouquet of flowers!

Potato Print Wrap

What You Need:

raw potato
knife
assorted miniature
   cookie cutters
pencil with eraser
tempera paint
white shelf or
   tissue paper

It's fun to make your own wrapping paper!

What You Do:

1. Cut the potato in half, carefully to give it a smooth surface.

2. Mark your design on the flat, cut side of the potato and then carve away the part you don't want to print. Or press a small cookie cutter into the potato -- this works very well. Keep the raised design simple for the best print.

Christmas trees, stars, holly, gingerbread dolls -- the possibilities are endless!

155

Here's a sample of
a design to try:

or you might
want to try
some of these...

Stamp holly leaf
in green a variety
of ways on your
paper.
When leaves are
dry use a potato
stem or eraser end
of pencil to stamp
holly berries.

156

Happy
"holly day"!

cookie cutter design

3. Blot away the potato juice.

4. With the brush, paint the cut surface of the potato with the tempera.

5. Press the potato design to print a variety of patterns on your paper. Use your creativity in placing your design to change the effect.

<u>What You Get:</u>

Your own individualized wrapping paper!

Or you might want to try a potato print greeting card!

"The whole earth has rest and is at peace..."

And now a gift <u>for</u> the garden...

Recycled Christmas Tree

Recycle your Christmas tree by putting it out in the garden when the holidays are over. The needles will fall off and become "natural" fertilizer for your garden.

In the spring you can trim off the branches and you'll have a sturdy stake for a new climbing vine plant.

The garden says "thank you"!

Herbs

Your indoor or outdoor grown herbs make delightful gifts!

Fresh Herbs

Share a little of your garden's wealth by giving a cluster of fresh herbs planted in an attractive container.

Tie a ribbon around it and make someone happy!

Dried Herbs

Herbs dried and stored in tightly sealed jars or packages make nice gifts as well.

Here's how to do it!

Cut plants off near soil level.

Remove heavy stems and spread the rest to dry on a window screen or piece of screening.

Store in a dark place.

Every few days check the leaves to see if they crumble when you rub them between your fingers.

Push herbs through a coarse sieve. You may pack each herb separately or mix them to blend flavors.

Be sure to label each one with the name of the herb!

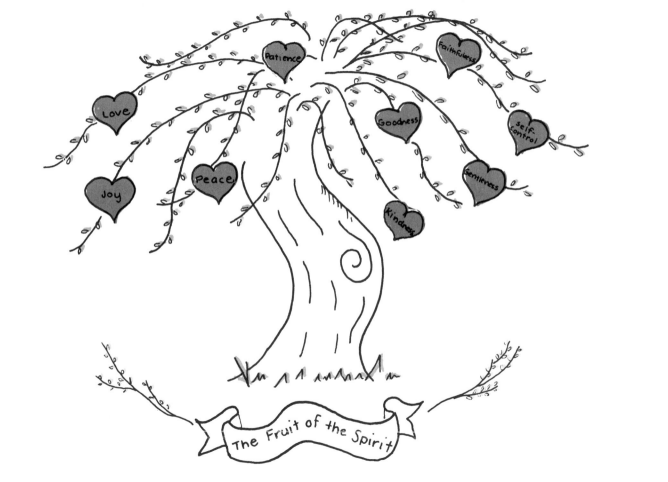

Resources: for families who want to know more

| Seed Catalogs |

W. Atlee Burpee
P.O. Box 6929
Philadelphia, PA 19132

Roswell Seed Company
P.O. Box 725
Roswell, NM 88201

Farmer Seed and
        Nursery Company
Faribault, MN 55021

Parks Seed Company
Greenwood, SC 29646

Gurney Seed and Nursery
        Company
Yankton, SD 57078

| World Food Needs |

Bread for the World
6411 Chillum Place, N.W.
Washington, D.C. 20012

CROP
P.O. Box 968
Elkhart, Ind. 46514

Church World Service
475 Riverside Drive
New York, N.Y. 10027

Mennonite Central Committee
21 South 12th Street
Akron, Pa. 17501
        or
201-1483 Pembina Hwy.
Winnipeg, Manitoba R3T 2C8

Magazines and Bulletins

Organic Gardening and Farming, Rodale Press,
   Emmaus, PA 18409

Superintendent of Documents
U.S. Government Printing Office
Washington, DC 202050

Recreational Community Gardening
U.S. Government Printing Office
Washington, DC 20402

Organizations

Gardens for ALL Inc.
Box 371
Shelburne, VT 05482

Local County Extension Office

Index

About the Authors...

Linda Hunt:

Presently the coordinator of the freshman writing program at Whitworth College, Linda is also a free-lance writer. Since graduating from the University of Washington, she has taught in junior and senior high schools, worked for the YWCA, and completed a Master's degree. She, her husband Jim, and their three children enjoy experimenting in their family garden with new crops. "Bok Choy was a disaster last summer, but spaghetti squash, yellow wax beans, and ornamental gourds produced beautifully!"

Marianne Frase:

During her twenty years as an elementary school teacher (in the San Francisco Bay Area, Princeton, Atlanta, and Spokane) Marianne has used her lettering and lady bugs to enhance the joy of learning for children. A graduate of the University of California at Berkeley, she also has a Master's degree in education from Whitworth College. She, and her husband, Ron, became acutely aware of world food concerns while in Brazil working with the United Presbyterian Church USA mission program. With their two college-age daughters they have enjoyed being part of a three-family garden where, with friends, they can share the work and rewards of gardening together.

Doris Liebert:

Doris attended Seattle Pacific University, after growing up in Calgary, Alberta. While working with Young Life in Pasadena, California, she met her husband Don, a student at Fuller Seminary. She stayed at home for several years while her children were young and gradually earned a Master's degree in early childhood education at Whitworth College. Presently, she is an instructor in the education department at Whitworth. Her son digs and prepares the garden, her daughters help to plant and weed, and all enjoy harvesting and eating the bounty!

♥ With "thank you" bouquets to...

...our husbands, for their encouragement and love

Jim, Ron, Don

...our "favorite local expert"

Jeanne Rees

...a talented Korean artist for his watercolor renditions of the cover and division page art

Seho Park

...and to our young artist friends:

Colleen Kelly - for her major artistic contributions to the book, cover and seasonal division pages, and 10, 15, 21, 22, 23, 29, 30, 34, 40, 57, 58, 65, 104, 127, 138, 154, 158
Susan Hunt - pages 11, 33
Lissa Marshall - page 19
Lynn Liebert - pages 20, 45, 75, 85, 98, 103, 113
Jill Marshall - pages 27, 79, 80, 91, 102, 115, 124
Adrian Balazs - page 40
Kate Herbig - page 46
Tara Emch - page 62
Serena Reidy - pages 55, 68, 89, 116, 118, 123
Krista Hunt - pages 65, 117
Stephanie Spencer - pages 71, 92

Adam McVay - page 87
Jenny Spencer - page 88, 96
Kerri Quai - page 95
Emily Bradford - pages 101, 142
Ricky Ferguson - page 126
Tammy Lattin - page 126
Mike Ferguson - page 140
Tad Heinen - page 143
Mindy Correll - page 164

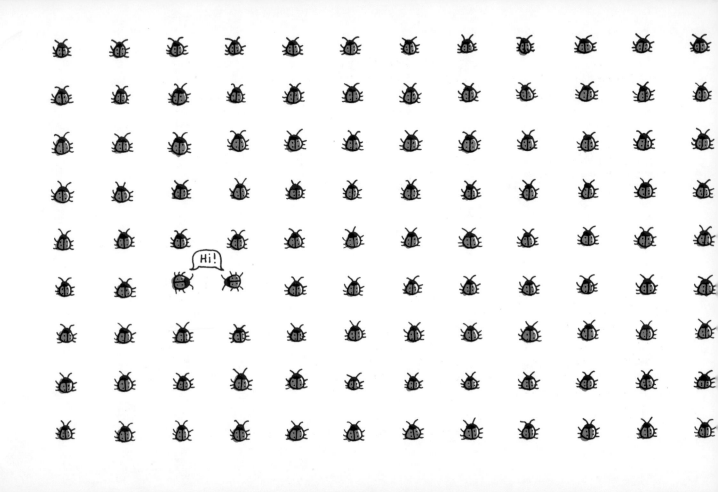